OPENING *Intuition* BOOK 3

DISCOVERING YOUR
PAST LIVES

AN EASY-TO-USE, STEP-BY-STEP ILLUSTRATED GUIDEBOOK

LUCY BYATT   KIM ROBERTS

FINDHORN PRESS

© LUCY BYATT & KIM ROBERTS 2016
THE RIGHT OF LUCY BYATT AND KIM ROBERTS TO BE IDENTIFIED AS THE AUTHORS
OF THIS WORK HAS BEEN ASSERTED BY THEM IN ACCORDANCE WITH THE
COPYRIGHT, DESIGNS AND PATENTS ACT 1998.

PUBLISHED IN 2016 BY FINDHORN PRESS, SCOTLAND
ISBN 978-1-84409-704-3

PROOFREAD BY NICKY LEACH
DESIGN BY LUCY BYATT
PRINTED AND BOUND IN THE EU

PUBLISHED BY FINDHORN PRESS
DELFT COTTAGE, DYKE,
FORRES IV36 2TF,
SCOTLAND, UK
TEL +44(0)1309-690582
FAX +44(0)131-777-2711
FINDHORNPRESS.COM
INFO@FINDHORNPRESS.COM

DISCLAIMER

OPENING2INTUITION, LUCY BYATT &
KIM ROBERTS, OFFER THEIR WORK FOR
YOUR PLEASURE & ENTERTAINMENT. AS
ARTISTS & CREATORS, WE BELIEVE THAT
THROUGH OUR OWN EXPERIENCES OUR
IDEAS ARE WORTHY OF PUBLICATION
& PRESENTATION. WE ADVISE YOU NOT
TO USE THIS WORK AS AN ALTERNATIVE
TO PRACTICAL MEDICINE OR MENTAL
& EMOTIONAL HEALTH CARE. WE ALSO
SUGGEST YOU DO NOT DRIVE DURING
OR IMMEDIATELY AFTER DOING ANY
OF THESE EXERCISES. HOWEVER WE
DO URGE YOU TO ENJOY, EXPAND AND
BECOME CONSCIOUS OF THE BEAUTIFUL
SPIRIT THAT YOU TRULY ARE.

CONTENTS

WE RECOMMEND YOU USE THE COMPANION
OPENING2INTUITION STARTER AUDIO-CD
WHEN YOU PRACTISE THE EXERCISES AND
VISUALIZATIONS DESCRIBED IN THIS GUIDEBOOK

TIP

ALL TEMPLATES IN THIS BOOK,
AS WELL AS IN BOOKS 2 AND 3,
CAN BE DOWNLOADED IN ONE GO AT
ganxy.com/i/111812

OUR INTENTION AT **OPENING2INTUITION** IS TO PROVIDE A SAFE AND SIMPLE WAY FOR PEOPLE TO OPEN UP TO THEIR INTUITIVE SELF. WE BELIEVE THAT EVERYONE CAN BE INTUITIVE AND DEVELOP THEIR PSYCHIC AND HEALING ABILITIES. IN FACT, THE PROCESS IS VERY SIMPLE AND NOT COMPLICATED AT ALL.

AT **OPENING2INTUITION** WE HAVE DEVELOPED A VISUAL PROCESS OF LEARNING THAT ALLOWS YOU TO SEE HOW ENERGY WORKS. THIS BOOK IS THE FOUNDATION OF A SERIES OF BOOKS THAT START WITH THE BASICS AND DEVELOP WITH EACH VOLUME. OUR AIM IS TO MAKE INTUITIVE WORK AVAILABLE TO EVERYONE AND TO TEACH IN WAYS THAT TARGET EVERYONE'S INDIVIDUAL LEARNING CAPABILITIES. ENERGY WORK IS NOT ALWAYS EASY TO UNDERSTAND. SOME PEOPLE DON'T NECESSARILY SEE THE ENERGIES AT WORK IN THE WORLD THAT PSYCHIC AND INTUITIVE PEOPLE ACCESS. THIS IS WHY WE HAVE CHOSEN TO MAKE THIS BOOK A VISUAL BOOK. WE WANT TO SHOW YOU HOW ENERGY WORKS, HOW VARIOUS PSYCHIC DEVELOPMENT EXERCISES WORK AND WHAT ACTUALLY HAPPENS WITH ENERGY WHEN YOU OPEN UP INTUITIVELY.

OPENING UP TO YOUR INTUITION SHOULD BE FUN. WITH THIS BOOK YOU CAN WORK AT YOUR OWN PACE, LEARNING THROUGH EACH OF THE CHAPTERS, BUILDING YOUR SKILLS. IT STARTS WITH THE BASICS AND DEVELOPS YOUR KNOWLEDGE THE FURTHER YOU GO THROUGH THE BOOK. THERE IS ALSO AN ACCOMPANYING CD DESIGNED AROUND THE EXERCISES IN THIS BOOK. THE CD HAS BEEN CO-CREATED WITH MUSICIAN, HEALER AND PSYCHIC KAREN GRACE. THE CD USES SPECIFIC SOUND VIBRATIONS TO OPEN AND EXPAND YOUR INTUITION IN NEW WAYS.

YOU CAN ALSO VISIT OUR WEBSITE TO LEARN MORE ABOUT OUR UPCOMING BOOKS, CDS AND TEACHING COURSES.

WWW.OPENING2INTUITION.COM

Kim Roberts and Lucy Byatt
X

FOR THE BEST EXPERIENCE POSSIBLE, WE SUGGEST YOU USE THE EXERCISES FROM BOOK 1 ('PSYCHIC DEVELOPMENT THE BASICS') TO FOLLOW OUR OPENING AND CLOSING TECHNIQUES.

EXCERPTS HAVE BEEN INCLUDED IN THIS BOOK TO GET YOU STARTED.

GROUNDING AND PROTECTION ARE VERY IMPORTANT WHEN FOLLOWING OUR PAST LIFE EXERCISES. THAT IS WHY WE HAVE INCLUDED SOME BASIC DIAGRAMS IN THIS BOOK THAT REFER BACK TO BOOK 1.

WE ALSO SUGGEST YOU USE THE VISUALIZATIONS WE HAVE PREPARED ON OUR 'OPENING2INTUITION STARTER AUDIO-CD'. THIS WILL ADD TO THE SUCCESS OF YOUR EXERCISES.

INTRODUCTION

PAST LIVES

AN INTRODUCTION

**PAST LIVES
PREPARATION
VISUALIZATION**

**DRAWING
CLOSING DOWN
GROUNDING**

PAST LIVES

AS YOU BEGIN TO OPEN UP TO YOUR INTUITION,

YOU MAY FIND THAT YOU BEGIN TO DEVELOP AN INTEREST IN PAST LIVES.

PAST LIVES ARE PREVIOUS LIVES THAT WE HAVE EXPERIENCED PRIOR TO THE LIFE WE ARE CURRENTLY LIVING.

THE ESSENCE OF WHO YOU ARE.....

YOUR SOUL

IS ON A SPIRITUAL JOURNEY WHERE IT WILL CHOOSE TO HAVE MANY DIFFERENT LIFETIMES.

EACH LIFETIME WILL PROVIDE A DIFFERENT EXPERIENCE AND LESSON.

IT IS THROUGH THIS CONTINUATION OF LIVES THAT OUR SOUL LEARNS AND EVOLVES.

AND YES WE HAVE ALL HAD MANY, MANY LIVES....

AS WE BEGIN TO OPEN UP INTUITIVELY WE BECOME MORE AWARE OF OUR SOUL'S JOURNEY.

THIS MAY LEAD TO A GREATER UNDERSTANDING OF WHY WE ARE HERE AND WHAT WE ARE DOING.

AS THIS AWARENESS OPENS UP TO YOU...

WOW! HAVE WE MET BEFORE? I RECOGNIZE YOU FROM SOMEWHERE!

YOU MAY REMEMBER A PLACE FROM THE PAST, OR PERHAPS A PERSON.

HELLO! IT'S LOVELY TO MEET YOU.

IT'S FUNNY. I FEEL AS IF I'VE KNOWN YOU FOREVER!

THEY MAY SUDDENLY BECOME FAMILIAR TO YOU.

YES, I WAS JUST SAYING THAT TO GABRIELA!

THIS IS BECAUSE YOU MAY BE IN THE SAME SOUL GROUP.

I FEEL VERY HAPPY AND COMFORTABLE IN BOTH YOUR COMPANY!

KEEPING AN OPEN MIND IS IMPORTANT WHEN EXPLORING YOUR PAST LIVES.

MOST OF US HAVE EXPERIENCED SOME KIND OF EMOTIONAL TRAUMA IN A PAST LIFE.

WE CAN LOOK AT THEM THROUGH OUR VISUALIZATIONS AND EXPLORE THE DRAMA SURROUNDING OUR PAST LIVES.

BUT THOSE FEELINGS AND SCENARIOS DO NOT BELONG IN OUR PRESENT LIFE.

SO MANY LIVES. EXHAUSTED. MUST SLEEP!

Z
Z
Z

IT IS IMPORTANT TO EXPLORE WHO WE ARE NOW, AND WHO WE HAVE BEEN, SO THAT WE MAY UNDERSTAND OURSELVES BETTER IN THIS WORLD.

OUR REALITY IN THIS LIFE IS THE MOST IMPORTANT REALITY. WE STRONGLY SUGGEST THAT YOU KEEP THIS IN MIND AS YOU DISCOVER YOUR MANY PAST LIVES.

INTRODUCTION TO PAST LIVES

PART 1 **EXPLORING OUR PAST LIVES**

PREPARATION

CLEANING

AS A STARTING POINT, WORKING IN A CLUTTERED SPACE WILL NOT BE GOOD FOR YOU.

IT IS IMPORTANT TO SET ASIDE A CLEAN AND CLUTTER-FREE SPACE TO WORK IN.

BUT IT'S NOT JUST THE PHYSICAL CLUTTER WE NEED TO ATTEND TO.

SMUDGING

TAKE YOUR SMUDGE STICK AND LIGHT IT WITH A CANDLE.

OR USE ANY ROOM CLEANSING TECHNIQUE YOU MAY KNOW.

1 ALLOWING THE SMUDGE STICK TO SMOULDER.

2

THEN BLOW OUT THE FLAME

AFTER MOVING THROUGH THE ROOM WITH YOUR SMUDGE STICK, OPEN ANY WINDOWS AND ALLOW THE SMOKE TO CLEAR.

INTENTION

BY STATING OUR INTENTION WE EMPOWER THE RITUAL OF SMUDGING AND ENFORCE WHAT IT IS THAT WE PLAN TO DO.

MY INTENTION IS TO CLEAR MY SPACE OF ANY NEGATIVE UNWANTED ENERGY. THIS IS IN PREPARATION FOR ME TO MEET ONE OF MY PAST LIVES. MEETING THIS PAST LIFE SHOULD BE RELEVANT TO MY LIFE AT PRESENT AND BE A HEALING EXPERIENCE.

INTENTION IS VERY POWERFUL!

GET YOUR DISC READY

TRACK 7

THE PAST LIFE VISUALIZATION IS ON TRACK 7 OF THE OPENING2INTUITION STARTER AUDIO-CD OR MP3.

OPENING2INTUITION STARTER CD IS AVAILABLE FROM YOUR LOCAL BOOKSHOP OR FROM WWW.FINDHORNPRESS.COM WHERE YOU WILL ALSO FIND A DOWNLOADABLE MP3 VERSION.

WE HAVE WORKED WITH SINGER AND PSYCHIC KAREN GRACE TO GET THE RICH POWERFUL SOUND THAT WILL TRANSPORT YOU VERY QUICKLY TO THAT ALL-IMPORTANT PAST LIFE!

PREPARATION

LOOK INTO BOOK 1 ('PSYCHIC DEVELOPMENT THE BASICS') FOR DETAILED PREPARATION, GROUNDING, CLEANSING AND PROTECTION EXERCISES.

PROTECTION

ENERGY

CLEANSING

GROUNDING

CHAKRAS

CROWN

THIRD EYE

THROAT

HEART

SOLAR PLEXUS

SACRAL PLEXUS

BASE

'OPENING UP' IS ABOUT RAISING SPIRITUAL VIBRATION TO A HIGHER LEVEL THROUGH THE CHAKRAS

RESEARCH AND GET TO KNOW THE MEANING OF EACH CHAKRA IN YOUR BODY.

WE HAVE A CHAPTER IN BOOK 1 ('PSYCHIC DEVELOPMENT THE BASICS') THAT WILL INTRODUCE YOU TO A BASIC UNDERSTANDING.

Chak·ra: NOUN

PREPARATION

PREPARATION

 **KEEP YOUR EYES CLOSED.**

FOCUS ON THE BREATH. VISUALIZE BREATHING IN A SENSE OF CALMNESS. AS YOU EXHALE LET GO OF ANY TENSIONS IN THE OUT-BREATH.

EXPAND

EXPAND THE COLOURS OF YOUR ENERGY AS FAR AS YOU CAN.

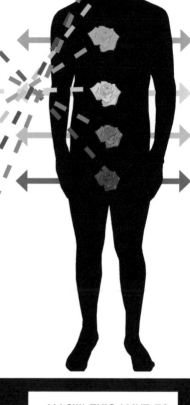

 SLOWLY TURN YOUR FOCUS TO YOUR BASE CHAKRA. VISUALIZE A RED FLOWER IN BUD. SLOWLY OPEN THIS FLOWER, DRAW IN ENERGY THROUGH THIS CHAKRA, OPENING EACH CHAKRA AS YOU GO.

 MOVE UPWARDS THROUGH THE CHAKRAS INTO THE SACRAL CHAKRA.

 MOVE UPWARDS THROUGH THE CHAKRAS INTO THE SOLAR PLEXUS.

 MOVE UPWARDS THROUGH THE CHAKRAS INTO THE HEART CHAKRA.

 MOVE UPWARDS THROUGH THE CHAKRAS INTO THE THROAT CHAKRA.

 MOVE UPWARDS THROUGH THE CHAKRAS INTO THE THIRD EYE CHAKRA.

 MOVE UPWARDS THROUGH THE CHAKRAS INTO THE CROWN CHAKRA.

IMAGINE BREATHING IN VIBRANT BRIGHT WHITE LIGHT.

ALLOW THIS LIGHT TO ENTER YOUR BODY.

BREATHE OUT ANY TENSIONS, THEN REPEAT THE PROCESS, INHALING BEAUTIFUL WHITE LIGHT INTO THE BODY.

LET IT CLEANSE AND CLEAR ANY NEGATIVE FEELINGS OR STRESS FROM THE BODY.

PREPARATION

VISUALIZATION

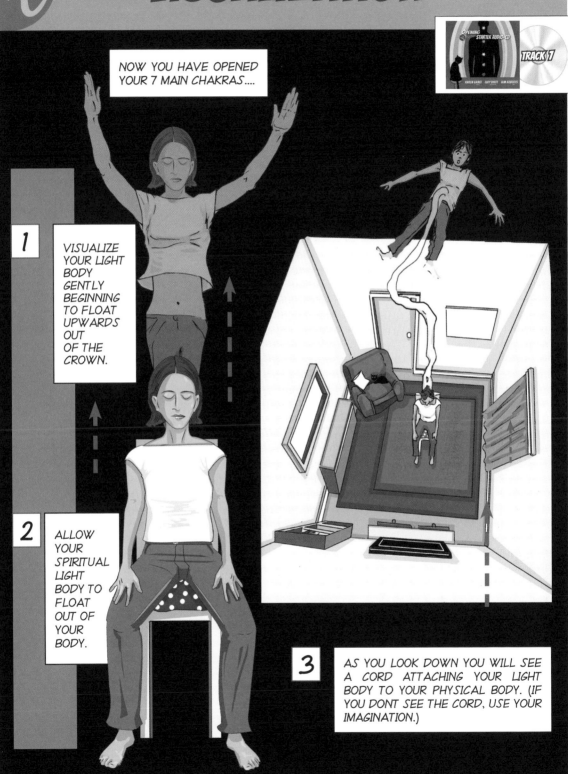

NOW YOU HAVE OPENED YOUR 7 MAIN CHAKRAS....

1 VISUALIZE YOUR LIGHT BODY GENTLY BEGINNING TO FLOAT UPWARDS OUT OF THE CROWN.

2 ALLOW YOUR SPIRITUAL LIGHT BODY TO FLOAT OUT OF YOUR BODY.

3 AS YOU LOOK DOWN YOU WILL SEE A CORD ATTACHING YOUR LIGHT BODY TO YOUR PHYSICAL BODY. (IF YOU DONT SEE THE CORD, USE YOUR IMAGINATION.)

ALLOW YOURSELF TO FLOAT UPWARDS INTO THE SKY.

SEE YOURSELF FLYING UP THROUGH THE CLOUDS,

UP INTO SPACE AND FINALLY INTO THE HEAVENS.

AS YOU REACH THE HEAVENS NOTICE A GOLDEN GATE.

FLY TOWARDS THIS.

AT THE GOLDEN GATE

ONE OF YOUR GUIDES WILL BE WAITING FOR YOU.

GREET YOUR GUIDE AND THANK THEM FOR COMING.

TELL THEM THAT YOUR INTENTION IN COMING HERE IS TO JOURNEY INTO ONE OF YOUR PAST LIVES.

ALLOW YOUR GUIDE TO LEAD YOU THROUGH GOLDEN GATE AND TO THE TOP OF A BEAU GOLDEN STAIRWELL.

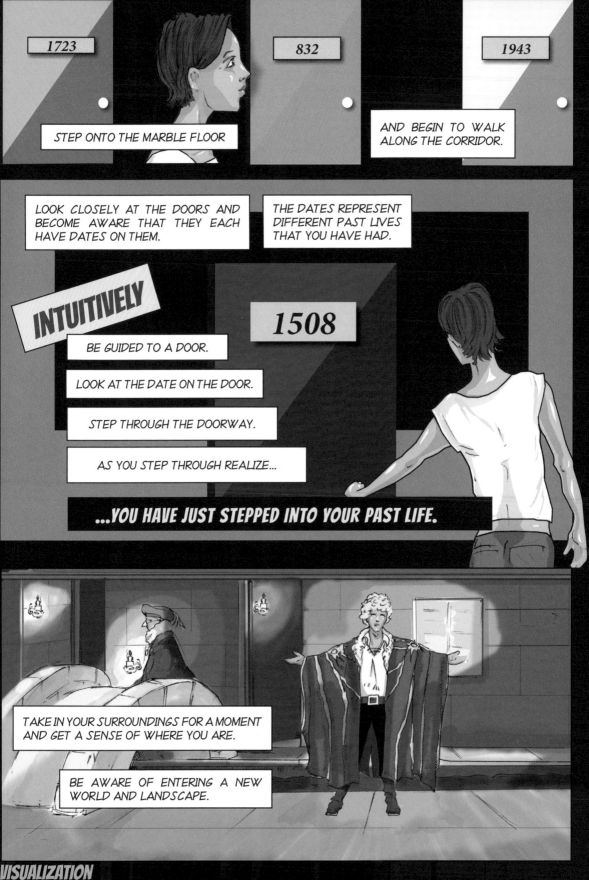

VISUALIZATION

NOTICE THE CORD ATTACHING YOUR LIGHT BODY TO YOUR BODY.

MOVE YOUR LIGHT BODY BACK INTO YOUR PHYSICAL BODY.

ALLOW YOUR LIGHT BODY TO MERGE BACK WITH YOUR PHYSICAL SELF.

SLOWLY BEGIN TO BECOME AWARE OF YOUR BODY AGAIN.

WIGGLE YOUR FINGERS.

WIGGLE YOUR TOES.

SLOWLY

AND COME BACK INTO YOUR ROOM.

VISUALIZATION

KEEP YOUR EYES CLOSED.

FOCUS ON THE BREATH. VISUALIZE BREATHING IN A SENSE OF CALMNESS. AS YOU EXHALE LET GO OF ANY TENSIONS IN THE OUT–BREATH.

CONTRACT

CONTRACT THE COLOURS OF YOUR ENERGY INTO YOUR CHAKRAS.

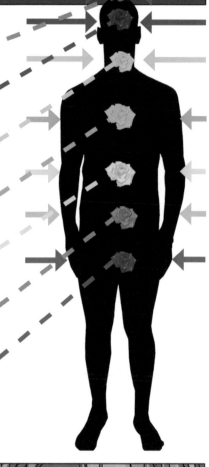

 FOCUS ON CONTRACTING THE ENERGY BACK INTO EACH CHAKRA, CLOSING THEM LIKE FLOWERS. MOVE DOWNWARDS THROUGH THE CHAKRAS, STARTING FROM THE CROWN CHAKRA.

 MOVE DOWNWARDS THROUGH THE CHAKRAS, CLOSING THE THIRD EYE.

 MOVE DOWNWARDS THROUGH THE CHAKRAS, CLOSING THE THROAT CHAKRA.

 MOVE DOWNWARDS THROUGH THE CHAKRAS, CLOSING THE HEART CHAKRA.

 MOVE DOWNWARDS THROUGH THE CHAKRAS, CLOSING THE SOLAR PLEXUS.

 MOVE DOWNWARDS THROUGH THE CHAKRAS, CLOSING THE SACRAL CHAKRA.

SLOWLY TURN YOUR FOCUS TO YOUR BASE CHAKRA. VISUALIZE A RED FLOWER, FINALLY CLOSING DOWN THIS LAST CHAKRA.

BRING YOUR FOCUS TO YOUR FEET

1 IMAGINE ROOTS COMING OUT OF THE SOLES OF YOUR FEET INTO THE GROUND.

2 VISUALIZE YOUR ROOTS GROWING AND MOVING DOWN THROUGH THE FLOOR AND INTO THE EARTH.

3 MOVING DEEPER, THROUGH THE LAYERS OF THE EARTH....................

.....UNTIL YOU REACH THE CENTRE OF THE EARTH.

4 AT THE CENTRE OF THE EARTH, IMAGINE A GIANT GREEN CRYSTAL.

VISUALIZATION

5 WRAP YOUR ROOTS AROUND THIS GREEN CRYSTAL.

FEEL YOUR CONNECTION TO THE EARTH STRENGTHEN.

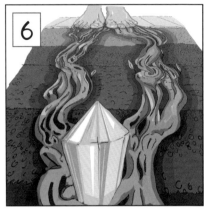

6

VISUALIZE DRAWING ENERGY FROM THE GREEN CRYSTAL INTO YOUR ROOTS.

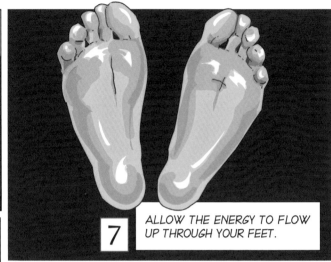

7 ALLOW THE ENERGY TO FLOW UP THROUGH YOUR FEET.

8 BRING THE ENERGY UP YOUR LEG

9 BREATHE IN BREATHE OUT

10 HOLD THAT ENERGY IN YOUR HEART CHAKRA.

11 OPEN YOUR EYES.

12 BECOME AWARE OF YOUR SURROUNDINGS.

VISUALIZATION

DRAWING

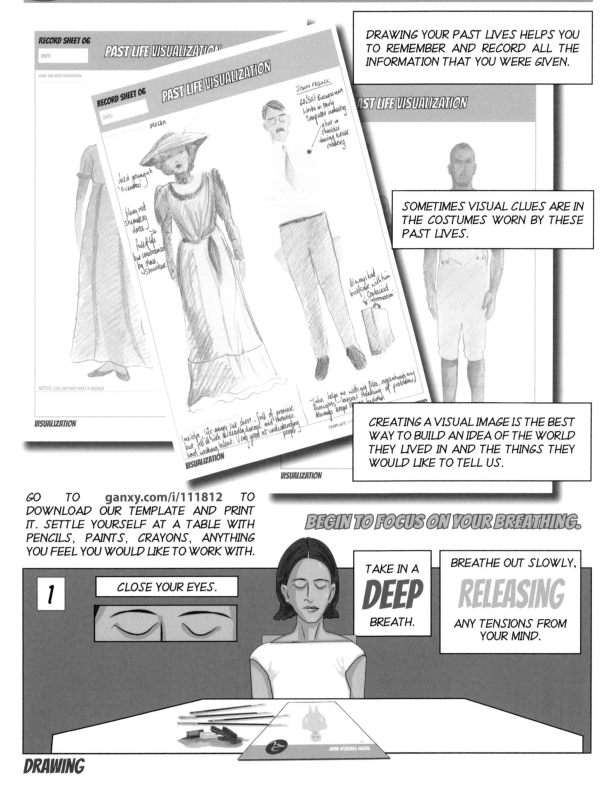

DRAWING YOUR PAST LIVES HELPS YOU TO REMEMBER AND RECORD ALL THE INFORMATION THAT YOU WERE GIVEN.

SOMETIMES VISUAL CLUES ARE IN THE COSTUMES WORN BY THESE PAST LIVES.

CREATING A VISUAL IMAGE IS THE BEST WAY TO BUILD AN IDEA OF THE WORLD THEY LIVED IN AND THE THINGS THEY WOULD LIKE TO TELL US.

GO TO ganxy.com/i/111812 TO DOWNLOAD OUR TEMPLATE AND PRINT IT. SETTLE YOURSELF AT A TABLE WITH PENCILS, PAINTS, CRAYONS, ANYTHING YOU FEEL YOU WOULD LIKE TO WORK WITH.

BEGIN TO FOCUS ON YOUR BREATHING.

1

CLOSE YOUR EYES.

TAKE IN A **DEEP** BREATH.

BREATHE OUT SLOWLY, **RELEASING** ANY TENSIONS FROM YOUR MIND.

DRAWING

SET YOUR INTENTION.

MY INTENTION IS TO REMEMBER AND RECORD ALL THAT I EXPERIENCED DURING MY PAST LIFE VISUALIZATION.

AS THIS GUIDE BEGINS TO COME FORWARD, ALLOW THEM TO BLEND WITH YOUR AURA AND ENERGY.

1 FOCUS ON THE GUIDE YOU MET IN YOUR GUIDED PAST LIFE VISUALIZATION.

2 BECOME AWARE OF ANY SENSATIONS COMING IN AS YOUR GUIDE DRAWS CLOSER.

3 REMEMBER THE EMOTIONS OF THIS PAST LIFE AND HOW THEY UNFOLDED IN FRONT OF YOU.

4 REMAIN DETACHED FROM NEGATIVE EMOTIONS, BUT REMEMBER AS MUCH INFORMATION AS YOU CAN.

5 YOU WILL BE WRITING THESE DETAILS DOWN, AS WELL AS DRAWING WHAT YOU SAW, SO TAKE A MOMENT TO REFLECT ON YOUR JOURNEY.

6 BEFORE YOU LEAVE THIS LIFE, ALLOW YOURSELF TO FEEL YOUR PAST LIFE IN YOUR ENERGY FIELD.

7 YOU MAY WORK WITH THIS PAST LIFE FOR MANY DIFFERENT REASONS IN THE FUTURE. SO REMEMBER THEIR ENERGY AND HOW IT FEELS TO YOU.

8 THEY MAY LEAVE CLUES OR SENSATIONS IN YOUR BODY SO YOU CAN RECOGNIZE THEM IN THE FUTURE.

DRAWING

9 OPEN YOUR EYES.

RETURN YOUR FOCUS TO THE PAST LIFE VISUALIZATION MAP.

USING YOUR COLOUR PENCILS/ CRAYONS, BEGIN TO COLOUR IN THE COSTUME OR OUTFIT YOUR GUIDE WAS WEARING.

AS WELL AS DRAWING THE PAST LIFE, YOU MIGHT WANT TO WRITE IN SOME WORDS DETAILING WHAT YOU FELT FROM THIS LIFE.

10 FILL IN AS MUCH DETAIL AS YOU CAN.

ALWAYS DATE AND NAME YOUR LIVES.

KEEP ADDING TO THE INFORMATION AS YOU REMEMBER IT, BUILDING UP A DETAILED PROFILE THAT YOU CAN REFER BACK TO WHEN NEEDED.

REPEAT THE PROCESS WITH YOUR OTHER PAST LIVES WHEN YOU ARE READY. THIS WILL SHOW YOU HOW EACH INDIVIDUAL LIFE LINKS TO YOU AND WHY. BY USING THE PAST LIFE VISUALIZATION TEMPLATE YOU CAN BUILD YOUR OWN LIBRARY OF HISTORY AND KNOWLEDGE.

DRAWING

PAST LIFE VISUALIZATION

RECORD SHEET

TODAY'S DATE:

DATE **1508-ish**   AGE **17-18?**

WHO WERE YOU (BRIEF DESCRIPTION) Ricardo, Artist — *Name or description*

TIME PERIOD/PLACE Medieval Italy – Venice, Florence

FEMALE ○   MALE ✓

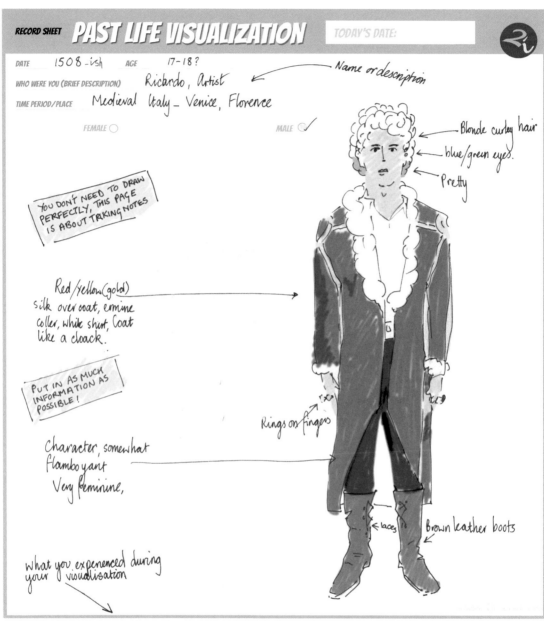

— Blonde curley hair
— blue/green eyes.
— Pretty

YOU DON'T NEED TO DRAW PERFECTLY, THIS PAGE IS ABOUT TAKING NOTES

Red/yellow(gold) silk over coat, ermine coller, white shirt, Coat like a cloack.

PUT IN AS MUCH INFORMATION AS POSSIBLE!

Rings on fingers

Character, somewhat flamboyant Very Feminine,

laces

Brown leather boots

What you experienced during your visualisation

SUMMARY: *(USE ANOTHER SHEET IF NEEDED)* Son of rich merchant, Painter, fascinated by the magic of the moon. Lost male friend to murder. Watched him being stabbed in a boat on a venice waterway. Wrapped in carpet and thrown into the water. Threatened by his killer <u>never</u> to set foot in Venice again or would suffer the same fate. (Spared because his father, a rich prominent businessman made a deal with the murderer.) Had to hide out for the rest of his short life as the killer had family all over Italy. They were under orders to kill on sight.

LESSON: *(WHAT DO YOU THINK THIS LIFE WAS TRYING TO TEACH YOU?)* Talents, hidden, fear of exposure. Unable to feel comfortable in recognition.

this may change, and alter, but you can re-write and add later as you like (on an extra piece of paper.

DRAWING

RECORD SHEET 07

PAST LIFE VISUALIZATION

NAME AND BRIEF DESCRIPTION

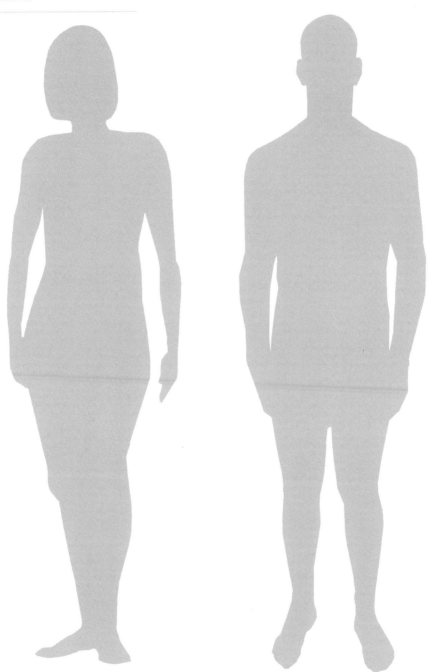

NOTES: (USE ANOTHER SHEET, IF NEEDED)

FINDHORN PRESS

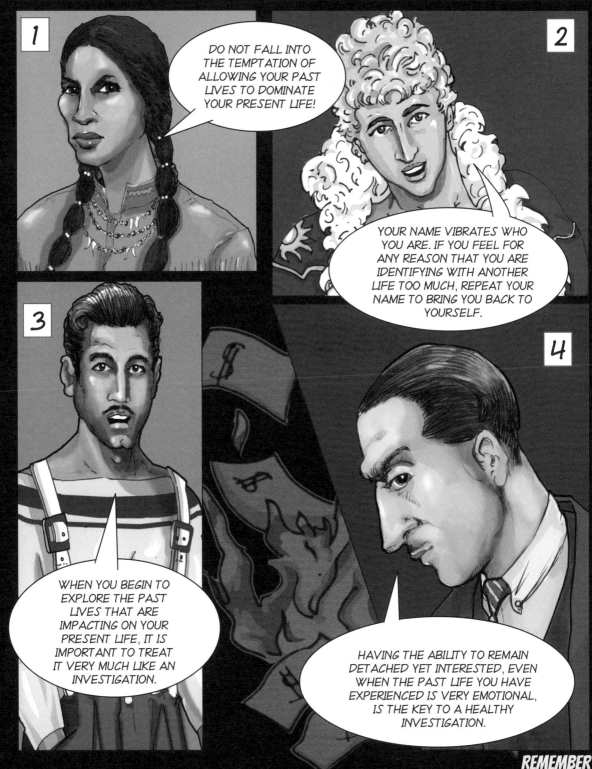

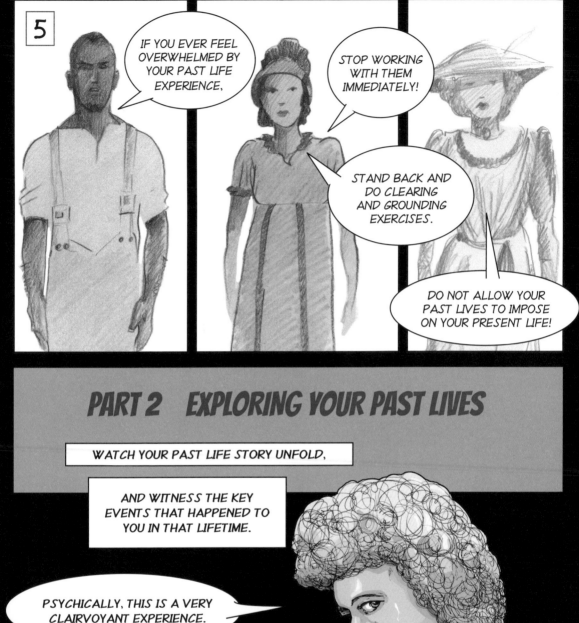

PART 2   EXPLORING YOUR PAST LIVES

PAST LIFE CASE STUDY

BEFORE WE VENTURE INTO ANOTHER ONE OF YOUR PAST LIVES, LET'S RUN THROUGH AN EXAMPLE OF HOW THIS ALL WORKS.

CLAIRE HAS BEEN HAVING SOME RELATIONSHIP PROBLEMS.

CLAIRE

CLAIRE HAS MADE A DEEP CONNECTION WITH JORDAN.

JORDAN

JORDAN AND CLAIRE HAVE BEEN DATING FOR A FEW MONTHS.

SHE FEELS LIKE SHE HAS ALWAYS KNOWN HIM BUT FINDS IT HARD TO TRUST HIM AND OFTEN FINDS HERSELF WITHDRAWING FROM HIM.

SHE DECIDES TO GET A PAST LIFE READING TO SEE IF SHE CAN GAIN SOME UNDERSTANDING INTO WHAT IS HAPPENING TO HER.

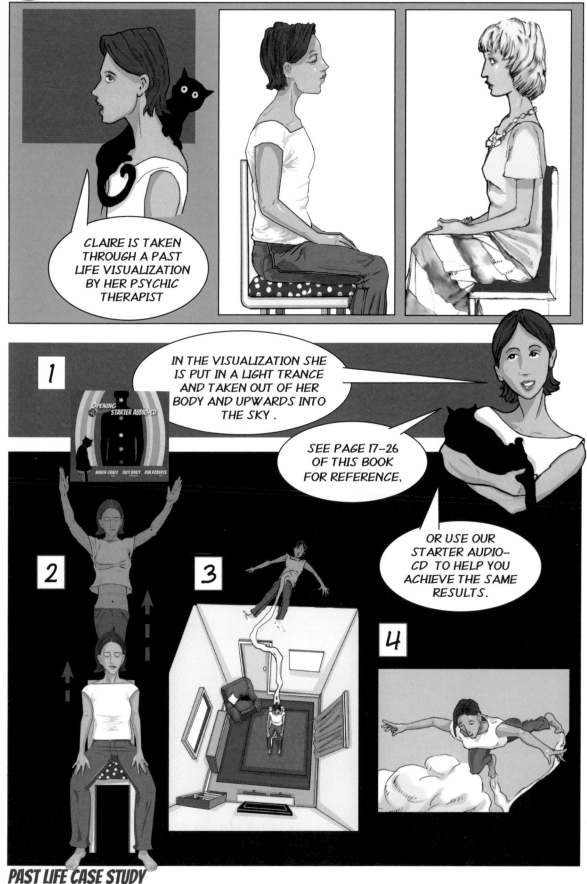

WHO AM I?

LOOK AT YOUR FEET AND DESCRIBE THEM.

LOVELY SHOES WITH A NICE BOW AT THE FRONT.

MY BEST SHOES, WHICH I WEAR WHEN I TRAVEL OR GO TO CHURCH.

PAST LIFE CASE STUDY

JULIETTA AND LUCA HAVE LEFT THE RESTRICTIONS OF POVERTY AND THE GROWING FASCIST RIGHT WING MOVEMENT IN 1920S AND 1930S ITALY.

THEY ARE SEEKING A BETTER LIFE IN NEW YORK.

LUCA'S COUSIN DANTE LIVES IN LITTLE ITALY ON THE LOWER EAST SIDE.

THEY ARE GIVEN A ROOM IN LUCA'S COUSIN'S HOUSE. DANTE TAKES LUCA UNDER HIS WING. HE FINDS HIM A JOB WORKING FOR A 'RESPECTABLE' BUSINESS MAN.

JULIETTA IS OBLIVIOUS TO THE DANGERS OF LUCA'S EMPLOYMENT POSSIBILITIES.

SHE IS FULL OF AWE IN THIS LAND OF OPPORTUNITY.

PAST LIFE CASE STUDY

44

THE BOSS IS REALLY IMPRESSED WITH LUCA.

Silvio

HE QUICKLY CLIMBS THE LADDER IN HIS JOB.

WE GET OUR OWN HOUSE AND CAR.

LIFE IS HAPPY AND I THINK LUCA IS MAKING AN HONEST LIVING.

EVERYONE IS VERY GLAMOROUS.

LUCA OWNS HIS OWN CLUB NOW.

LUCA HAS LOTS OF FRIENDS AND ADMIRERS.

GET THE SINGER A BOTTLE OF CHAMPAGNE, COMPLIMENTS OF THE HOUSE!

YES, SIR

THEN LUCA BECOMES A DAD.

PAST LIFE CASE STUDY

PAST LIFE CASE STUDY

BACK IN THE ROOM

NOW WE BEGIN TO BRING CLAIRE BACK INTO THE ROOM.

1

SHE IS ASKED TO COME BACK OUT THROUGH THE DOOR.

2

UP THE STAIRS

3

AND FLOAT DOWN THROUGH THE SKY

4

BACK DOWN INTO HER BODY.

5

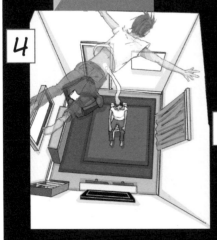

SHE IS DIRECTED TO GROUND HERSELF BEFORE SHE OPENS HER EYES.

SHE FEELS ROOTS GROW IN HER FEET.

6

THE ROOTS COME FROM HER SOLES RIGHT DOWN INTO THE CENTRE OF THE EARTH.

BACK IN THE ROOM

DISCOVERING THE MEANING OF YOUR PAST LIFE

NOW IT IS TIME FOR YOU TO EXPLORE ONE OF YOUR PAST LIVES.

TO REFRESH YOUR MIND, YOU CAN REFER BACK TO THE ORIGINAL PAST LIFE VISUALIZATION ON PAGE 18.

YOU CAN USE THE PAST LIFE REGRESSION TRACK (#7) ON THE 021 STARTER AUDIO-CD IF YOU WANT.

BREATHE **IN**

BREATHE **OUT**

Find Helpful techniques in our basics book

CALM THE BREATH AND CLEANSE THE LIGHT BODY.

EXPAND YOUR CHAKRAS.

LEAVE YOUR BODY UP THROUGH YOUR HEAD

ALLOW YOURSELF TO FLOAT UPWARDS INTO THE SKY.

MEET YOUR GUIDE AT THE GATE

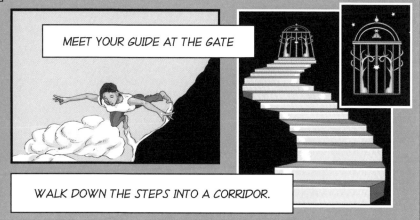

WALK DOWN THE STEPS INTO A CORRIDOR.

RECORD SHEET 08

DATE:

PAST LIFE WORKSHEET 1   WHO AM I?

1 PICK A DOOR. WALK UP TO IT.
LOOK AT THE DATE ON THE DOOR.
REMEMBER THIS FOR LATER.

2 GO THROUGH THE DOOR.

3 WHO AM I?
LOOK AT YOUR FEET.
LOOK IN YOUR MIRROR.
SEE YOUR FACE.
ASK YOURSELF YOUR NAME,
AGE AND NATIONALITY.

4 WHERE AM I?
LOOK AROUND YOU.
WHERE ARE YOU?
IN THE CITY OR IN THE TOWN?
NEAR THE BEACH OR IN THE DESERT?
BEGIN TO BUILD A PICTURE OF THE
SETTING YOU FIND YOURSELF IN.

5 TAKE YOUR TIME TO EXPLORE
THIS LIFETIME.
WITNESS THE KEY EVENTS.
TAKE AS LONG AS YOU NEED.

6 COME BACK TO THE ROOM.
GROUND.

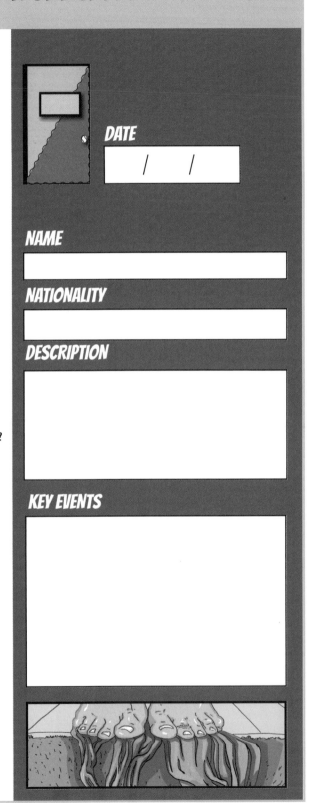

DATE

/   /

NAME

NATIONALITY

DESCRIPTION

KEY EVENTS

RECORD SHEET 09

DATE:

PAST LIFE WORKSHEET 2 WHO AM I?

NOW YOU HAVE DISCOVERED A NEW PAST LIFE, LET'S EXPLORE AND RECORD WHAT HAPPENED IN THAT PAST LIFE.

USE THE TEMPLATES OR TAKE A BLANK SHEET TO DRAW YOUR PORTRAIT.

DRAW YOUR FEET/SHOES/FOOTWEAR

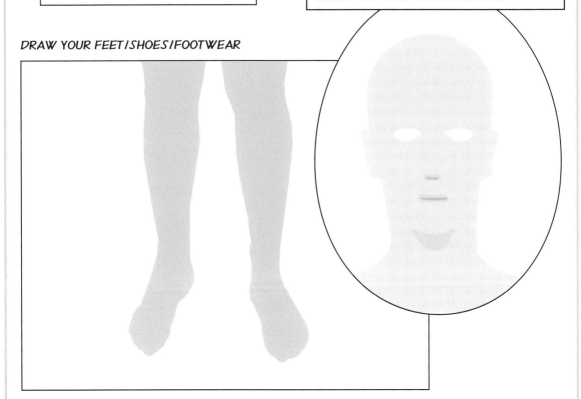

DRAW IMMEDIATE SURROUNDINGS. TOWN/CITY/COAST. LOCATION IN THE WORLD. NIGHT/DAY.

FINDHORN PRESS

RECORD SHEET 10

DATE:

STORYBOARD EXAMPLE   MY STORY

STORYBOARDING YOUR PAST LIFE

TO MAKE SENSE OF YOUR PAST LIFE, A GOOD EXERCISE TO DO IS CREATE A STORYBOARD SHOWING THE MAIN EVENTS OF YOUR PAST LIFE.

A STORYBOARD IS A BIT LIKE A COMIC BOOK PAGE WHERE YOU DRAW IN BOXES EACH EVENT AS IT HAPPENS. THESE IMAGES CAN THEN BE READ IN SEQUENCE TO CREATE A MINI STORY.

LOOK AT THE EXAMPLE OF JULIETTA'S STORYBOARD AND THEN TRY TO CREATE YOUR OWN, USING THE STORYBOARD TEMPLATE.

DISCOVER THE MEANING OF YOUR PAST LIFE

RECORD SHEET 10

DATE:

STORYBOARD TEMPLATE MY STORY

NOW YOU HAVE YOUR STORYBOARD, RE-READ IT AND TAKE A MOMENT TO THINK
WHAT IS THE LIFE LESSON THAT YOUR PAST LIFE IS TRYING TO TEACH YOU.

WORKSHEET 4
MY PAST LIFE LESSON IS:

CLOSING DOWN

AFTER OPENING UP TO DO ANY PSYCHIC WORK, IT IS IMPORTANT THAT WE CLOSE DOWN.

WE MUST MAKE SURE THAT WE ARE GROUNDED AND PROTECTED FROM ANY NEGATIVE ENERGIES IN OUR ENVIRONMENT.

1

CLOSE YOUR CHAKRAS

CONTRACT

CONTRACT THE COLOURS OF YOUR ENERGY INTO YOUR CHAKRAS

USE THIS TECHNIQUE TO CLOSE ALL YOUR CHAKRAS

PLACE A GOLDEN BALL OF LIGHT OVER EACH CLOSED CHAKRA.

2 GROUND YOURSELF

IMAGINE ROOTS COMING OUT OF THE SOLES OF YOUR FEET INTO THE CENTRE OF THE EARTH.

VISUALIZE DRAWING ENERGY FROM THE GREEN CRYSTAL INTO YOUR ROOTS.

ALLOW THE ENERGY TO FLOW UP THROUGH YOUR FEET.

AT THE CENTRE WRAP YOUR ROOTS AROUND A GREEN CRYSTAL.

3 VISUALIZE YOUR PROTECTIVE CLOAK OR ARMOUR.

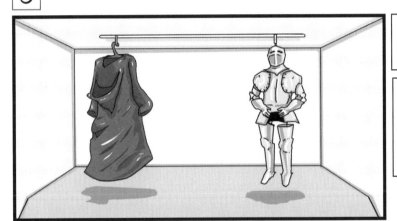

AFTER CLOSING DOWN, IT IS ADVISABLE TO WEAR YOUR CLOAK OF PROTECTION.

THIS WILL PREPARE YOU ENERGETICALLY TO GO BACK INTO THE WORLD AND DO YOUR NORMAL EVERYDAY THINGS.

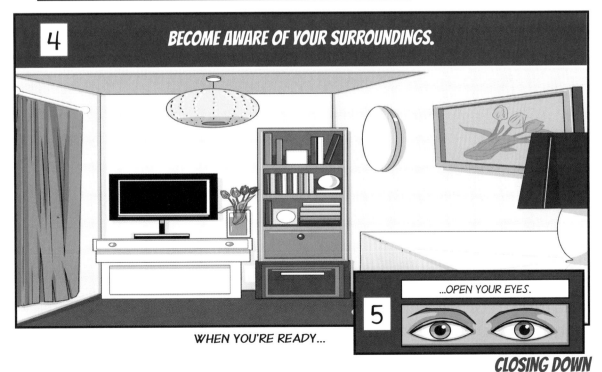

CLOSING DOWN

WEBSITE/COURSES

WEBINARS

MENTORING

DEVELOPMENT CIRCLES

ONLINE

COURSES

VIDEOS

WORKSHOPS

CDS

1:1 TEACHING

IF YOU ARE INTERESTED IN DEVELOPING YOUR INTUITION FURTHER, PLEASE COME AND VISIT OUR WEBSITE.

WWW.OPENING2INTUITION.COM

ON OUR WEBSITE YOU WILL DISCOVER MANY ADDITIONAL RESOURCES, INCLUDING ONLINE TEACHING COURSES AND MP3 DOWNLOADS.

WE WILL ALSO KEEP YOU UP TO DATE WITH THE PROGRESS OF OUR NEXT BOOK, TEMPLATES, DOWNLOADS AND CDs IN THE OPENING2INTUITION SERIES.

COME AND JOIN US AT THE CREATIVE PLACE TO DEVELOP YOUR INTUITION.

WEBSITE/COURSES

TEMPLATES

ALL 11 TEMPLATES IN THIS BOOK, AS WELL AS IN BOOKS 1 AND 2, CAN BE DOWNLOADED IN ONE GO AT ganxy.com/i/111812

BIOGRAPHIES

KIM ROBERTS WRITER

IS A PSYCHIC CLAIRVOYANT AND HEALER WITH 16 YEARS' EXPERIENCE IN PSYCHIC READINGS AND TAROT. SHE IS A FULLY QUALIFIED REIKI MASTER AND NLP PRACTITIONER.

KIM WORKS AS BOTH A READER AND A TEACHER, AND HAS RUN NUMEROUS HEALING AND PSYCHIC DEVELOPMENT WORKSHOPS OVER THE PAST FEW YEARS IN THE UK.

KIM RUNS AN ONLINE PSYCHIC DEVELOPMENT GROUP FOR CELEBRITY PSYCHIC MICHELE KNIGHT ON A WEEKLY BASIS. KIM HAS A B.A.HONS DEGREE IN ENGLISH AND PSYCHOLOGY AND IS A WRITER INTERESTED IN EXPLAINING AND DEVELOPING THE EASY UNDERSTANDING OF ENERGY AND THE NATURE OF HEALING.

LUCY BYATT ILLUSTRATOR

IS A PSYCHIC ARTIST WITH NEARLY 30 YEARS' EXPERIENCE IN SPIRITUAL TRAINING, HEALING, REIKI, MEDIUMSHIP AND PSYCHIC DEVELOPMENT. SHE HAS TAKEN MANY COURSES AT THE COLLEGE OF PSYCHIC STUDIES IN LONDON AND HAS WORKED AS A PSYCHIC ARTIST WITH VARIOUS COMPANIES, DOING READINGS, DEMONSTRATIONS AND TALKS.

LUCY ALSO WORKS WITH AUTISTIC CHILDREN AND MENTORS CHILDREN IN SCHOOLS IN 'DANGER OF EXCLUSION', AS WELL AS STUDENTS INTERESTED IN PSYCHIC AND COLOUR DEVELOPMENT, LUCY HAS FACILITATED A NUMBER OF WORKSHOPS AT THE ISBOURNE FOUNDATION IN CHELTENHAM, TEACHING COLOUR AND PSYCHIC ART.

LUCY GRADUATED WITH A B.A. HONS 1ST DEGREE IN FINE ART FROM GOLDSMITHS ART COLLEGE, AND HAS AN M.A. IN SCULPTURE FROM THE UNIVERSITY OF GLOUCESTERSHIRE. SHE HAS MANY YEARS' EXPERIENCE AS A FREELANCE ILLUSTRATOR AND GRAPHIC DESIGNER WORKING FOR NUMEROUS BUSINESSES. LUCY HAS EXHIBITED HER SCULPTURES AT THE FLORENCE BIENNALE.

LUCY AND KIM BEGAN WORKING TOGETHER IN 2007, AND THROUGH TRANCE CHANNELLING WITH THEIR GUIDES, OPENING2INTUITION CAME INTO EXISTENCE.

ACKNOWLEDGEMENTS

THANK YOU

OPENING2INTUITION WOULD LIKE TO THANK THEIR SPIRIT GUIDES FOR PROVIDING DETAILED CHANNELLED INFORMATION FOR THIS BOOK.

WE WOULD LIKE TO THANK KAREN GRACE FOR COMING ON BOARD AND GETTING INVOLVED WITH OPENING2INTUITION. SHE HAS PROVIDED SOME SPECTACULAR MUSIC AND VOCALS FOR OUR CDS. KAREN HAS ALSO PUT IN NUMEROUS LENGTHY SKYPE CONFERENCE CALLS AND IS A VALUABLE MEMBER OF OUR TEAM.

WE WOULD LIKE TO THANK CAROLYN FINLAY FOR PROOREADING THIS BOOK. THANK YOU, YOUR MANY HOURS DOTTING I'S AND CROSSING T'S OVER THE WONDERS OF THE TELEPHONE WERE INVALUABLE AND ENJOYABLE.

WE WOULD LIKE TO THANK CHRISTINE MITCHELL FOR LENDING US HER MUSICAL EAR TO LISTEN TO THE FINAL CHECKS FOR THE CD. THANK YOU, YOUR INPUT AND TIME WAS MUCH APPRECIATED.

WE WOULD LIKE TO THANK KATHRYN TRAYNOR, OLWEN TRINGHAM, DENISE RUTTER AND LIZ HILLIES FOR TAKING TIME OUT OF THEIR BUSY SCHEDULES TO PROOFREAD THE BOOK AND LISTEN TO FINAL CHECKS AROUND THE CD.

WE WOULD LIKE TO THANK OUR READERS FOR BUYING THE BOOK, AND HOPE THAT OUR WORK ENABLES YOU TO OPEN UP TO YOUR INTUITION IN NEW AND EXCITING WAYS.

WE WOULD ALSO LIKE TO THANK OUR FAMILIES AND FRIENDS WHO HAVE BEEN PATIENT AND UNDERSTANDING OF THE WORK AND TIME WE HAVE NEEDED TO DEDICATE TO MAKING THE COMPLETION OF THIS BOOK POSSIBLE.

Kim Roberts and Lucy Byatt
X